MW01096376

ISBN-10: 1475174993
ISBN-13: 978-1475174991

Biography

Marki Costello, the self-proclaimed and widely acknowledged "Queen of Hosting," is a highly respected and well-established name in Hollywood.

Owner and president of Creative Management Entertainment Group, Marki has single-handedly built the most respected host management company in the industry. CMEG has flourished since its creation more than a decade ago. Originally the only host management firm in town, the company has expanded to encompass a casting division, a production arm, a huge hosting school and a website devoted to hosting, www.becomeahost.com.

A strong gene pool may have been a defining influence insofar as her career direction. Marki's grandfather was comedy legend Lou Costello of Abbott & Costello, and her father – Gregg Jacobson, was a record producer for The Beach Boys. Growing up as Hollywood royalty, Marki appropriately became a multi-hyphenate in today's television industry.

With a rapid-fire delivery, quick wit and professional style, Marki Costello has earned a reputation as being a straightforward and tenacious dealmaker. Her undeniable charisma and larger-than-life personality have also made her a regular on television shows over the years. She was the star of her own show on TV Guide Network's *Open Call*, a reality show which followed Marki as she cast 10 different shows. She's also appeared as a co-host with Danny Bonaduce on VH-1's *I Know My Child's a Star*, a judge on Joel Silver Productions' *Next Action Star*, and a judge on E!'s *Fight for Fame*.

For the past 10 years, Marki has worked as a casting director for major network studios including Disney, Warner Bros., FOX, and TBS. She began casting classic reality and game shows before anyone knew just how big "reality" TV was going to become – including casting the first season of ABC's *The Bachelor* and Fox's *Temptation Island*. She has also cast for such shows as NBC's *Meet My Folks,* Fox's *Man Vs. Beast,* NBC's *Next Action Star,* Fox's *Looking for Love: Bachelorettes in Alaska*, Fox's *Surprise Wedding I* and *II, The Newlywed Game, The Dating Game, Hollywood Squares,* and *Love Connection*. In addition to reality casting, Marki has also cast numerous host roles, including the host and co-host position for Oprah's OWN Network game show, *Are You Normal, America?* She also did the casting for the host position for The Travel Channel's *World Poker Tour*, The Learning Channel's *Tabloid Busters*, and The Food Network's *Cupcake Wars*, to name a few. She also did a nationwide casting search for TV Guide Network's *Hollywood 411* correspondent position, and REELZ Channel's search for a new on air correspondent. With an impressive list of credits and amazing ability to bring "the best" to the table, it's no wonder that the *Los Angeles Times* has touted Marki as, "One of the world's most prized talent scouts!"

Marki's company, CMEG, specializes in the management of over 30 on-air hosts, including Jason Kennedy of E! News, television's Katie Wagner, host Debbie Matenopoulos, and Emmy® Nominated game show host Todd Newton, host Rossi Morreale, and on air correspondent Marc Istook.

In addition to casting and management, Marki also puts her talents to work by teaching one of the most prestigious on-camera host seminars in the country, "Become A Host." Based on referrals from networks, top Hollywood agents, casting directors and production companies, her monthly "boot camps" have been consistently booked full since their inception. Marki's Hosting School also offers weekly ongoing classes to her students, taught by some of the most renowned producers, agents, hosts, and TV executives in Hollywood. Additionally, Marki has been involved with various workshops around the country, including one for the American Film Institute.

W Magazine ran a feature on Marki's Hosting Boot Camp in its September 2007 Issue. Writer Kevin West stated, "[The boot camp] promises an introduction to this ever expanding sector of the entertainment industry-a strange, quasi-journalistic beat where going behind enemy lines means crossing the velvet rope to get the real inside dish from all your favorite celebrities."

Marki has also worked on major branding campaigns for top Hollywood professionals and personalities, including writer Stephen Cannell (*The A! Team*), E! star Dr. 90210, and Frank Yang, president and owner of Simple Human.

One wouldn't be remiss in naming Marki as the "Jack of All Hollywood Trades."

Forward

This book is for anyone who wants to make it in the world of hosting, and that is a very big world. I remember sitting in a meeting at ABC about ten years ago, and the conversation was about reality television – everyone in the meeting was calling it a fad. They thought it would come and go, just like everything else in television. Well, cut to ten years later and reality is not a fad - nor is it going away.

The networks love reality television because it's inexpensive to produce. Think about it: They don't have to really pay the "talent" (compared with the fees actors get on scripted shows). The contestants are free! So all that leaves with regards to who gets paid is the host(s) and/or experts. And here's the good news: You no longer have to be a traditional host like Ryan Seacrest to get a big hosting job on TV. You can be a designer, a chef or a hairstylist - and voila! You are now hosting your own show. Take Dan and Dean, they are twin brothers known as "D" Squared." They are from Canada and live in Rome, Italy, and are huge designers. When Bravo was looking for a new host for their show "Launch My Line," they did at first see traditional hosts. But ultimately the network executives passed on all of them, because they realized they wanted the hosts for this particular show to be experts in the field. So they looked at many designers and decided on "D Squared." I coached these brothers every day on the set of "Launch My Line" to get them ready to be on camera. I got them comfortable and helped them learn the ins and outs of connecting with their audience,

And that's when it dawned on me: I need to write this book. I have a wealth of information that I share exclusively with my clients and my students. But now it's time to share it with anyone who wants to be a host, and wants to know what they're getting themselves into before launching full steam into this line of work. And I have to ask you this question: Why would you want to learn from some out of work host, or a local news reporter/anchor who worked in one small market? These people can't get themselves on television, so how are they going to get you on TV? I mean no disrespect - but I do have to question why you would possibly want to take a "how to host" course from someone who tried to do it themselves and failed. It's important to learn from someone who knows this world from every angle. I know it from casting. I know it from managing. I know it from hosting myself - and I know it from teaching everyone you see on TV, from Kelly Osbourne to Cee Lo Green, from Whitney Cummings to Jason Kennedy, and from Hank and Kendra Baskett to Audrina Patridge. Remember: the hardest thing to book is a job. Once you have a job, you'll have producers, directors, hair and makeup people – a whole team devoted to helping you be the best you can be. I'm here to help you book that job.

This book is for all of you experts in your field, or the "next" Ryan Seacrest, or any of you out there who see yourself on TV but you're not sure how to do it. There's so much room for "Every day people" on television these days. Even professionally trained actors, who three years ago would have considered hosting "beneath them," are now looking to host shows, because they see that that's where the opportunity really lies right now. This book is also for the frustrated actor who might need to learn to paint with a different color. Or the hair stylist who wants to be the next Tabatha from *Tabatha's Salon Takeover*. Or the therapist who wants to be the next Dr. Phil. Or the local news anchor who wants to learn how to break into a big market and be the next Billy Bush or Chris Harrison.

I like to call hosting "The great balancing act." A good host connects with their audience, comes across as an expert and an authority, and acts naturally while also maintaining a sense of enthusiasm and professionalism. This book will teach you how to balance all of that, and thus help you become the best host that you can possibly be.

CONTENTS

ACKNOWLEDGMENT

I want to give a special thank you to my clients of past, present and future, along with my Become A Host students of past, present and future. You are the proof that if you practice what I preach, you will meet your goals and succeed in the world of hosting. In turn, without all of you, this book would not exist. You have inspired me to put my love and knowledge for this business into readable words. (Is readable a word ??? LOL) xoxo Marki

CHAPTER ONE:

THE 10 MISTAKES PEOPLE MAKE IN TV HOSTING

Everyone makes mistakes. Beginners do it. Pros do it. You see it happen all the time, during live broadcasts when there are no re-takes. When you're live, whatever you do, whatever you say, it all happens on the air and there are no "Take Backs." You're stuck with it. Then all you're left to do is cross your fingers and hope it doesn't end up on Youtube, making a mockery of the career you're trying so hard to build.

But that's live television. What about when it comes to hosting a taped show? Well my friends, I'm here to tell you: you have no excuse. You've had time to do the research. You know your subject. You most likely know your copy and what's expected of you on camera. You get the chance for a second take. And even a third take. Yet mistakes still get made. And PS – when you do make a mistake (which we all do because we are human), it's not about your fumble. It's how you recover your fumble. If it stops you dead in your tracks then you were never there to start! You can learn to stay connected to your audience and plow through your fumble because it's not about you, it's about your audience. And here's a tip: They are going to like you more if you stay connected to them and get back to business by recovering from your fumble. But if you can't recover, or if you ask to start over, or if you just seem completely lost, then obviously they're not going to like you, because you're just completely stuck in your own head.

Here are ten mistakes I'm going to help you avoid making.

1. It's not about you.

This is the most common mistake that hosts make. They take what they're reading, and make it about themselves, instead of who it's really supposed to be about: the audience. Being a successful host means connecting with your viewers. Networks base a show's "success" on how many people are watching: The more, the better. The more people who watch, the more money they can charge advertisers to air the program, and the more life that particular show will have. To be a successful host, you need to PLUG INTO YOUR AUDIENCE. Who is watching? Why are they watching? What information are they looking to get from me? Am I just standing here, reading what's in front of me, or am I connecting with them? Am I reading a story or TELLING a story? Am I giving them a reason to watch me as opposed to watching someone else? When you are able to answer these questions confidently, you are able to be a better host. The greatest hosts of TV have always put their audience first. I remember watching Oprah on her *Behind The Scenes* show on the OWN network. Producers would come into a pitch meeting with their ideas for new episodes of *Oprah*, and she would automatically say things like, "My audience will hate that," or "My audience is not interested in that." Never did she say "I don't want to do that," or "I don't care about that." It wasn't about her. It was about her audience. And if anyone can make it about "her," it's Oprah! She was so big and so widely respected with such a huge audience, that she could have done whatever she wanted. But she never lost sight of who it was really about: her audience.

2. You're not balancing the elements.

When you're hosting a show, there are a lot of things going on, and there's a lot you have to balance. Prompter. Co-host. Props. Audience. You could possibly be on location, you may be on a studio set, there may be an audience, you may be standing at a table, holding different items and talking about them. Perhaps you have a co-host with whom you're sharing the space, or the set, or the props. One of the biggest mistakes that hosts make is when they fail to balance all of these elements. It takes time, practice, skill and energy. Hosting is the great balancing act, and I'm going to help you learn how to balance the elements, and just as important – how to define what the elements are.

3. Your personality doesn't shine through

When you're standing on a set, those lights come on, the camera is rolling, and there is a stage crew around you - it's a lot of pressure. How do you maintain your sense of self (ie, what got you the gig in the first place) while also not being affected by everything surrounding you? This book will help you stay focused on who you are and how to keep your personality and point of view without being distracted by everything going on around you. This is where you need to balance!

4. You are reading a story instead of telling a story.

There's a big difference between telling a story and reading one. Think about the way you tell your friends when you have big news to share. Are you excited? Animated? Smiling? Of course you are. You wouldn't tell them the story flatly, as if to say "The sky is blue." You would be filled with excitement and emotion. Throughout this book we will help you learn how to get familiar with telling a story as opposed to reading a story.

5. You aren't coexisting with your co-host.

What happens when you are sharing the space on camera with another host? That's called co-hosting, but it may as well be called "coexisting" because that's what you have to do: coexist with someone else! You need to acknowledge the person standing next to you, listen to them when they talk (and not just wait for your turn to speak), and engage with them as well as the audience.

Did you catch those three important words?

- acknowledge

- listen

- engage

Coexisting falls under the "great balancing act" I spoke about. It's not just about you now, it's about building a chemistry with the person standing next to you so that you come across as a TEAM. Remember Season 1 of *American Idol*? Ryan Seacrest had a co-host. His name was Brian Dunkleman. Don't remember him? Then let that be a lesson right there.

6. You aren't listening

Hosts often make the mistake of not listening to the very people they are talking to. When you watch Ryan Seacrest interview some Idol hopefuls - you can tell he is listening to what they're saying and then he's asking FOLLOW UP questions that truly show a connection. When you ask someone, "How are you?" and they respond, "Not great, I haven't slept in weeks," Your follow-up question would be something along the lines of "That's awful, why can't you sleep?" But many hosts make the mistake of following up with a question along the lines of "How excited are you to be here?" Or whatever question was next on their pre-prepared list. This is a very common mistake made by hosts. In this book I am going to help you learn how to listen and respond, which will only make you a better interviewer, and better host. And wouldn't your audience think it's crazy if your cohost said "I had a horrible day," and you responded with "I'm so excited to be here!" Your audience would think you're crazy, selfish and insecure.

7. You don't have a brand

The future is here and that future is a world where everyone is a brand. Whether you want to be an entertainment news host or do a gardening show on HGTV, you need to have a brand. What is your expertise? What are you the most passionate about? This book will help you explore and figure out exactly what your brand is. That's what buyers are looking for. They want you to be someone with a point of view and a legitimacy that makes sense to their viewers. This doesn't mean you'll be pigeonholed into only working on one type of show, or as one type of person. But when you have a BRAND, you can speak about what you know best. This is how you get your big break – because you break where you have the most strength. Buyers can see you in that light and think, "He's great at talking about swimming / horticulture / fashion! Let's bring him in for our Olympics / Gardening / Designer show!" You may be surprised to read this, but when you speak about something you know, whether it's how to build the best play-yard or give the best first date advice, you will always be your most natural self, because it's EASIER to talk about what you know than what you don't know. This is part of why building your brand is so important. It puts you in your best light. You'll break where you have the most strength. For example, let's take Ty Pennington. His "break" came when he was given a show on TLC called *Trading Spaces*. That little show sparked major national interest, and Ty, building on what he knew best (how to work with his hands), parlayed that show into *Extreme Makeover: Home Edition,* on ABC (thrusting him from a small cable channel onto a major TV network). And after 200+ episodes, where is Ty now? He's a co-host on the new talk show, *The Revolution*. Not bad for a set designer who wanted to be on TV. And keep in mind, for some people, their brand is just their mouth. Seriously! Look at Chelsea Handler. She has made a spectacular career out of the things that come out of her mouth. She's a comedian, yes – but she's a talk show host. And she is, most importantly – herself. A potty-mouthed, no-filter, brash talker.

8. You have a brand, but you don't know how to market yourself

Now that you've established your brand, how are you going about marketing yourself? Do you have a website? Are you tweeting? Are you making webisodes and blogging on a weekly basis? Becoming a host takes WORK, and being a successful host means working even harder. In this book you will learn the value and importance of branding, marketing yourself and getting yourself out there. And if you are calling yourself a news junkie or a sports junkie or a fashion junkie, you better be up on every single thing in that world, every single day. You don't want to brand yourself as a something that you're not legitimately passionate about, or it will become painfully obvious during your first talent meeting. Do your homework! Fifteen minutes a day, getting up to speed on the latest news in your brand is all it takes to keep you at that "expert / junkie" level. That's it. Four years ago, hosts didn't have the same opportunities that they have today, with the internet, new media, social media, etc. You have no excuse not to succeed.

9. You don't have an *ism*

In hosting, your opinion equals your personality equals your "ism" (for example if I walk into an audition and they say, "I really need to see your personality!" – they want to see my *Marki-ism*). When someone is trying to direct you on camera to have more "personality," the mistake many hosts make is that they just try to make their read bigger, louder or more obnoxious. That's not "personality" - that's just obnoxious. It's important for you as a host to learn how to bring your personality forward – meaning your *isms* – your point of view – so that buyers can see exactly who you are and what makes you different, unique and special. Throughout this book, you will learn the importance of bringing your personality to the forefront so that buyers know exactly who you are, and what makes you stand out.

10. You aren't making the most of what's available to you

 Four years ago, up and coming hosts had to literally knock on the doors of every agency in Hollywood and New York, begging someone, anyone to look at their reel, look at their press kit, etc. Fast forward to today, and it's a whole different ballgame. Now, you have the tools to do it all yourself and really put yourself out there. Buy your own domain name and then either learn how to build your website or pay someone to do it for you. It's your career – make the investment! By building a website, doing webisodes, writing blogs and tweeting, you are able to get your career up and running without having to wait for someone to "see promise" in you. Now you can take your brand, talk about it every day or every week and really build yourself up as an expert or junkie in your field, and use that to get your foot in the door. You can shoot your own webisodes every week, two weeks, or even every month. You can set up a twitter handle and tweet people to watch your webisodes, and ask your friends to retweet you, and build up a following organically. Now, you're doing the work, you're putting yourself out there, and you're legitimizing yourself. You have substance. You have context. You're talking about things that matter to you and putting your best self forward. Trust me when I tell you, this is the way things are done now. It's the future of Hollywood. The lesson here is, If you build it, they will come. I promise. One tweet a day based on your brand and point of view, one blog a week based on your brand and point of view, and one webisode a month based on your brand and point of view. Many people ask me, why do I have to blog if I'm doing webisodes? Why both? The reason is because through your blog, we can see if you can write, how you write, we can really get the best sense of your point of view. Plus, consistency is key. Think of Carrie Bradshaw, Candace Bushnell's character from *Sex and the City*. They created a hugely successful TV series and movie franchise, all based on her dating column that ran in *The New York Observer*. Buyers loved her brand. Find your inner Carrie Bradshaw, and the buyers will come.

CHAPTER TWO:

PLUGGING INTO YOUR AUDIENCE

The biggest misconception when it comes to hosting is that people think it's easy. They think, "Oh, I just have to read this little piece of paper to camera and Boom! I'm a host!" In some ways that's true. You just have to read that little piece of copy on that plain piece of paper to camera. Easy for some people, but not so easy for others. And if you are reading this right now, you are probably saying, "Yeah that's it - so why do I get so nervous and scared and then read too fast?" As we established earlier, hosting is the great balancing act. But before you can start balancing, you need to be able to recognize what the elements are so that you know just exactly what it is you're balancing.

What you're going to learn next is the intellectual aspect to hosting, and what tools you need to balance the next time you have a hosting opportunity. Good hosts know that when they book an audition, and all they have is a piece of copy in their hands, they need to answer many questions before they get in front of that casting director. Remember: recognizing the elements helps you balance them.

- What is the show about?

- Who is the show targeting?

- What is the concept of the show (game, talk, news, reality, etc)?

- Who is the network buying this particular show?

- What is their demographic/audience?

Here's the reason why these questions – and their answers - are so important: Let's say for instance you were going to have an opportunity to audition for a game show for Spike TV. Think about how helpful it would be to go into that meeting, armed with the knowledge that their average viewer is MALE between 18-49 years old. So now you know who you're going to be talking to, connecting with and attempting to engage during your audition. Next step: who specifically is the program trying to reach?

Obviously, if you are hosting a show on ESPN, you're speaking to sports fans. If it's a show on the FUSE Network, you're speaking to young music fans. If it's on Bravo, did you know that the median age of the Bravo audience is 40, mostly female, and has a higher disposable income? (as of available research for the Q4 2011).

What is the concept of the show? If it's a reality show and you're going in to read for host, what kind of show is it? Docu-series? Dramatic? Challenge? If these reality show genres sound foreign to you, it's time to get familiar with a little search engine called Google. Once you know the concept, you know who you are connecting to. If the network is being kept a guarded secret, you can still find out whether it's "major network" (meaning, ABC, CBS, NBC or Fox), or "major cable" (meaning, E!, Style, Bravo, USA, TBS). If they're not even revealing that information, then it's up to you to really glean the copy and see who they're targeting. It's easier than you think, and I'll show you some examples later in this chapter. But the point is, with a little research and thought, you can walk into that audition armed and ready. You now know who the audience is, who they're targeting, and what the show is.

I honestly think that there's only a handful of working hosts out there who actually think about who they are talking to when they read the copy. And those few good hosts are the ones who keep getting work, keep booking jobs, over and over again.

Now that you know who the audience is, it's time to *connect with them*. Isn't it easier to read copy for Fuse now that you know who you're talking to? Visualize yourself on a stage in front of hundreds of young music fans and tell THEM the story you're about to read on prompter. Suddenly, you're engaging and connecting. Exude the passion you know those music junkies feel every time they see a story about their favorite band. Think about how they're going to feel when they get this brand new information that only you have. Your read all of a sudden has depth and gravity. You're actually plugging into something real and tangible. This is more than half the battle to getting that job.

So let's go back to where we started:

- You get an opportunity to host/audition for a show

- You read and practice the copy (oh, the dreaded copy!)

- You get a general vibe of the creative.

- You learn which network is behind the show

- You research that network's demographics so you know who you're talking to

Now, you are ready for the next step: Making sure you hit all your transitions. If you are asking, "What's a transition?" Then you are definitely just starting out as a host - and that's okay - maybe even better, because you haven't been able to form any bad habits... yet.

When you look at your copy, you may have four or five different beats to hit.

First, there's the *Show Open*. Here you do the big hello and welcome to the show. Then you might be tossing to another host in the studio or out in the field, you might have to do a tease and then toss to a commercial break. All of those different turns you have to make are called transitions. Think of it as if you are the driver of the show. And just like when you drive a car, sometimes you speed up and sometimes you slow down. You put your blinker on when you need to turn; you nearly come to a stop when you have to make a hard turn. I know my analogies aren't traditional but stay with me. Just like when you're driving, when you're hosting a show, you don't want the people "following you" to get lost or confused. Your audience has to be able to follow where you're going.

For example, when you are at the top of the show (what we call the Open), you give a big welcoming "Hello." Remember: You need to always be thinking about what your audience is thinking. Picture them at home, on the couch, sitting there thinking, "Who is this person, what is this show?" That's why the big hello starts off with "I'm (insert your name) and this is (insert your show's name). Then you start teasing what you have coming up in the show. So moving from your hello, into your tease, you need to TRANSITION. You don't want to have the same intonation when you say "Hello," as when you say, "Coming up." Otherwise it sounds flat. Here's an example:

Hi everyone and welcome to Action TV, I'm your host, _____. (*as you say this, think of the audience saying, 'Who are you?'*) Tonight we take you behind the scenes of the fast and furious world of dirt bikes! (*As you say this, think of your audience thinking, 'what is this show and what am I going to see tonight?*) Meet the guys who get down and dirty, training for hours every day! Then later, we'll meet some very unexpected bungee jumpers! (*You should be saying this line as your audience is thinking, 'what else are they going to show tonight?)* These ladies love to let go and you'll see why. But first tonight, (*You should be saying this line as your audience is thinking, what am I going to see RIGHT NOW*) let's go live to my co-host _____ who is hanging out with some very bizarre sports enthusiasts! Jane?

Do you see how much balancing you need to do with all of that copy? There might be not a lot of copy but there is a lot going on. And not only do you have to keep anticipating what your audience is expecting, but you can't get stuck in your head while you're saying it – or everything you say loses all meaning and it just becomes white noise. In other words, you have to master the skill of balancing the elements so that you're still paying attention to the words coming out of your mouth! That sounds so simple and obvious, but it's one of the biggest mistakes hosts make! They can't stop thinking about making sure they're connecting and smiling and nodding to the point where they become totally disconnected from what they're saying. Don't let this happen to you!

Now, more on those TRANSITIONS.

The "open" is when you say hello and welcome everyone to Action TV and talk about the first big story of the night (Dirt Bikes). But then you start to talk about the bungee jumpers, that's a completely different topic and so you need a TRANSITION to help you transcend from one idea to the next so that your audience stays with you. How do you convey a transition in your read? By changing your inflection. If you start out with your voice a little higher when you are welcoming everyone to the show, then as you start to talk about another topic, your voice perhaps drops half an octave. Think about when you are telling a friend a story. You say "Mary Jane got an A in chemistry today! But she didn't do quite as well in English." Say those two lines out loud as if telling a friend. Can you see how your inflection changes as you move from the first, to the second thought? It's the same thing with the Action TV copy above. You are changing thoughts – you are changing gears - so you change inflection. Similarly, if you are tossing to a commercial break, for example:

Those stories and so much more are coming up tonight on Action TV, so stick around, we'll be right back.

This line of copy requires a button at the end. You need to button up your thought so that everyone understands we're going to a commercial break now. It may seem like it should be so obvious but I promise you - it's not. Try saying that line out loud. Did you end it sounding like a question, or like a statement? A common problem that many hosts make is that they end their statements as if they're questions. How many times have you heard a host say "We'll be right back?" where it sounds like there's a question mark dangling onto the end of their sentence? That's BAD HOSTING. Don't get into that habit. And if you already have that habit - end it right here and right now. The line should be read as an exclamation, with big energy. "We'll be right back!"

The bottom line is that when a good host comes into an audition, I can tell right away because (s)he asks, "Who is my audience, who am I talking to?" A lesser host walks into an audition and asks "Where's the copy? Is there teleprompter? Will there be cue cards? Are you taping this?" That's not to say those are bad questions, but they're not the most important factors. When you walk into an audition with confidence, knowing that all you really need to know is who you're talking to, then that shows through in your read.

CHAPTER THREE:

SEEING BEYOND YOU

One of the hardest parts of hosting is seeing beyond yourself (and the copy, and your insecurities and fears, and any other baggage you may be holding onto). You need to be able to actually speak to the "Junkie," as I like to call it, who is watching the show. The junkie is your audience. Is it a news junkie, a sports junkie, a gossip junkie -- whatever kind of junkie it is, you need to figure it out and then make sure that's who you're connecting with, and that's who you're plugging into. Because if you're not, you're doomed. Once you figure out who that junkie is, you need to visualize talking to them, and connecting with them, and then – and ONLY then --- it will never be about that horrible piece of paper with the "dreaded copy" on it.

The hosting world is rarely ever about the copy. It's about you, and what *you bring to the copy*. Plug into your audience and connect to the people who will actually be watching the show. Buyers hire hosts with whom their audience can relate and connect. Make the teleprompter your lover, brother and best friend, or, if it's easier for you - just pick one. The prompter is a tool to love, and it will help you see past the piece of paper, the cameras, the producers and the casting director, and help you to really connect to your audience.

This isn't to say you shouldn't learn the copy. You will definitely need to look at it, read it, read it out loud, look at it again, put it away, bring it back out, read it again, repeat. But what is important here, before all the reading and re-reading and practicing, is that you ask yourself: What specifically do I need to concentrate on? There is only one thing: The Junkie. Because if you don't, and you're over-rehearsed and you get every word "just right" and you smile and nod and wink at all the times you think you're supposed to, then you just failed, big time. No one has ever lost a job because they screwed up a few words of copy. But countless host hopefuls have lost a job for failing to connect to their audience. Producers and casting directors would rather hire someone who screws up the copy, but knows who they are as a host and how to plug into their junkie, over someone who hits it all perfectly but ends up so stuck in their own head making sure they hit every single word that they failed to connect to anyone. Don't let the copy wrap itself around you - wrap yourself around the copy. That really is the key to hosting.

I recently had a well known name come in for a show I was casting. I had the copy in the teleprompter for all of the prospective hosts. I asked this well known on-camera talent if he had looked over the copy, and what he thought of it. He said no, because he knew it would be on prompter and he didn't want to seem "rehearsed." While I understand where he was coming from, here's what he missed: By not looking over the copy, he had absolutely no idea what he was coming in to read. He didn't even know it was a game show! You might think this isn't the norm, but it happens way more often than you would think! The worst part of this situation was that he was coming in to read for a game show! With rules! With a co-host! With a panel and judges! There were so many elements to balance and this very talented man had absolutely no idea what was going on. So he missed out on an incredible opportunity to host a network game show. All because he didn't want to seem "rehearsed." And instead he was so unbelievably unprepared that he didn't even get a callback.

But that was his mistake, not yours. So let's get back to you. Now that you have plugged into your audience and figured out that it's not about you, let's figure out exactly who you are. It's important to realize that when you were selected to come in for an audition, it's because the producers or casting directors saw something in you that they thought would be good for this project. So they DO LIKE YOU. But -- who are you? If you were called into a talent meeting, (which sometimes happens before an audition and sometimes happens after, so that network executives can meet you and get to know you), are you polished and ready to sell yourself?

That's what I'm going to help you figure out right now. What are five things about your personality or life experiences that you, and you alone bring to your read? What makes you, YOU? Ryan Seacrest is a perfect example of a host with a brand that buyers get. Whenever Ryan hosts a show, he's always himself. We as the audience know what to expect from him. He goes beyond the lens and communicates directly with his audience. He's the same guy on his radio show as he is on *E! News* and on *American Idol*. You know exactly what you're going to get when you book Ryan Seacrest. He knows his audience, and they know him. There's never a surprise - he's reliable and he's consistent -- and that consistency is a key that many hosts do not have.

Some other hosts who fit that bill would be, you guessed it, some of the biggest names in television. Oprah, Rosie, Doctor Phil, Jerry Springer, even Maury Povich. They are so plugged into their audience that they become one of them. For example, take Jay Leno and David Letterman. You are probably a fan of one, but not likely a viewer of both. Their personalities are different, and thus their audiences are different. Both of them know how to connect to their audience – and the viewers know exactly what to expect each time they tune in. From the kind of jokes they'll hear during the monologue, to the types of questions that will be asked during the celebrity interviews -- the whole shebang.

Here is the real tip to being a great host: When you make your audience the star is when you really become the star. Remember that! Make the audience your number one priority, and you become the next big host, like Ryan and Oprah and the other big stars you've dreamed of becoming.

It is important to remember that this is no time to be humble! If you won a local news Emmy® (but you don't want to do local news anymore so you're hesitant to bring it up) – BRING IT UP. If you won a beauty pageant and then went on to mentor young girls for the next year – BRING IT UP. That sets you apart and makes you stand out. The more you work on answering the above questions, the more confidently you'll be able to handle that talent meeting, and the more likely you'll leave there with the executives excited about you and wanting more. And that is the only goal.

CHAPTER FOUR:

DISCOVERING YOUR BRAND

The future of television hosting is all about branding. Buyers are looking for people who have a point of view and a passion about something. Earlier, I gave you the example of Ty Pennington, a set builder who has gone on to create an amazing on-camera career. You can be the next Ty Pennington, but it starts with a brand.

Sometimes it's hard for us to figure out exactly what our brand should be. We want to seem versatile, we want to seem open to many different fields and opportunities. Don't worry about being pigeon-holed! Jason Kennedy is an *E! News* correspondent and host, with an expertise in celebrity news.

But he was cast as the host of *Dance Machine* on ABC. Why? Because the producers loved him as a host. It's that simple.

I have clients with specialties ranging from finance to dating, but they audition for everything in between. What happens when you have a brand is that you put your best face forward. When you're talking about something you're passionate about, you are at your best. When you have enthusiasm, passion, energy and authority on a topic, what more could you ask for? Isn't it easier to create your hosting reel based on you talking about topics of great interest to you, than to just read generic sports copy or generic game show copy? Does this make sense to you? Think about how animated you are when you're telling a story to a friend or loved one about something that you're passionate about. That's you at your best. Now take that story and put a camera on you while you're telling it, and we've got gold.

But how do you figure out what your brand is? It's not as hard as you think. Let's start by answering these questions:

What three things are you really good at?

1.

2.

3.

What are three things about you that most people do not know and wouldn't guess? Dig down deep.

1.

2.

3.

Name three important things that have happened in your life thus far. (This can be anything from winning a triathalon to losing a parent).

1.

2.

3.

Now, take a look at what you just wrote and it should start to get your engine churning and your creative juices flowing. You are going to want to keep coming back here and looking at your answers to the questions above as you start to create your host materials. In the host world, it's very important for you to be able to walk into a talent meeting and say I'm blank, blank and blank. This is why you want me over anyone else. You need to be able to explain exactly who you are, sometimes in less than 90 seconds. Network executives don't have time to hear your entire biography. They're likely not interested in hearing how you won a swim meet in Junior High or that you got the lead in the High School play. You need to hone in on the most important aspects of your life as well as the skills you have that would be interesting to the most people. What specifically makes you you, what makes you different and what makes you stand out in a crowd. This is your focus; this is your brand.

Once you've figured out exactly who you are, now you need to practice telling people. Grab a friend or a brother or a spouse - and a timer. Tell them about you, wonderful you and see if you got to all the important stuff in 90 seconds or less. Trust me, the executives in the talent meeting will decide what they want to ask you more about. They'll say something like "Tell me more about your trip to Bhurma where you helped build a well?" Or "What made you want to create your own webisodes about first dates?" As long as you walk in there with the ability tell your story naturally and concisely, while still exuding confidence (but not arrogance), they will ask you questions. Maybe even lots of questions. Some talent meetings last 20 minutes, others last two hours. Usually, the talent who hasn't gotten their biography down pat with exactly what they want to say, are the ones whose meetings last 20 minutes. Because after a whirlwind of gobbledy gook about where you grew up and then oh yeah I worked on the campus TV station, oh and I have 4 brothers, etc, leaves the other people in the room so exhausted that they're really not interested in hearing anything else.

Still unclear as to just who you are? Let's simplify it further. If you were going to appear on *Today* with Matt Lauer, what topic could you easily speak about for 60 seconds without even giving it a second thought? Is it gardening? Shopping? Sports? Now take that generic topic and hone it into something more specific. Have you mastered the art of gardening in small spaces? Do you know how to spot the hottest trends in fashion for under 50 bucks? Do you know everything there is to know about the NHL? Do you see where I'm going here? Even if you feel like there's nothing out there that fits you, there is. You just need to dig deeper. Answer the following questions and we'll start getting somewhere.

1. What are your hobbies? List them in order of importance.

2. What is one topic that, whenever you talk about it, you get excited/heated/passionate?

3. What piece of advice do your friends or loved ones seem to come to you for?

Now that you have the answers to these questions, you should see some key words popping off the page at you. What are those words? Are they part of a topic that you could easily do a little more research on and then enjoy talking about? Could you see yourself creating webisodes where you talk about that topic? Could you interview friends about it? Do you have enough to say about it that you could blog every week on the topic? If the answer is not YES to all of the above, you need to keep working. Because once you have those yeses, you've got yourself a brand.

Remember though, that it is two-fold. You can't just have a "Brand." Once you figure out your brand, your strength and your launching off pad, you need to marry that to your point of view within that brand. You can have the same brand as other hosts — and you will — but what will make you different, and what will make you stand out is your own point of view. Your opinions. Your personality. That's what makes you unique, and that's what can help make you a star.

CHAPTER FIVE:

COEXISTING (CO-HOSTING)

There are many different types of hosts, and many different shows to host, and a couple of different ways to approach them. In this chapter, we'll look at co-hosting and, more specifically, the dreaded co-host audition.

Co-hosting is tricky because you need to have chemistry, or to rephrase: You need to create chemistry. Don't get me wrong: Bad chemistry can sometimes be better than great chemistry, but having no chemistry at all is death. Many people who audition know that these co-hosting auditions can be very daunting, and sometimes very damaging. I specialize in this type of casting and you would be amazed at the many people who let someone else ruin their chance at getting a job. Great co-host chemistry examples would be Regis Kelly, Regis and

Kathy Lee, Johnny Carson and Ed McMahon, all the women of "The View," Howard Stern and Robin Quivers, and Jason Kennedy and Giuliana Rancic.

So what is it that makes these co-hosts have great chemistry? They listened to each other. They reacted to each other. They didn't step all over each other's copy. They engaged with each other as well as the audience at home. Balance! That is the key.

A prime example about co-hosting from my own personal experience as a casting director would be from when I cast the show, *Dinner and a Movie*, for TBS. We were doing the final callbacks for the network, and we brought back two guys and three girls. We did a sort of mix-and-match to figure out who had the best chemistry together. We brought in one guy and then one by one, brought in each of the three girls. Annabelle Gurwitch did the first test read with Paul Gilmartin, and you could tell that Paul found her annoying. To be truthful, so did I, and so did the rest of the network execs. But as they worked together, something just clicked with their funny disdain for each other. And BAM! Just like that -- there it was: Instant chemistry. Because even though Annabelle was perceived as "annoying," Paul used it to his advantage and reacted the same way the audience would at home.

The key information I want you to glean from this example is that what chemistry is really all about is you being you in the moment, and not being stuck in your head, stuck in the copy, stuck in the thought of "when is it my turn to read?" You want to really react to your co-host, in an organic way that doesn't come across as "acting like you're reacting." Does that make sense? Organic chemistry sounds like an oxymoron, but it's exactly what you need to nail the job. The hardest part about nailing a co-host audition is that you have no idea how good your co-host is going to be during the audition. Maybe the network has already locked in the other talent and now they're just looking to match him/her up with someone. Or maybe it's another person auditioning at the same time. Maybe it's the show's executive producer and so you're extra nervous about having witty banter with someone who could ultimately be your boss. Sometimes, no matter how hard you try to "act naturally," there's nothing you can do to make that chemistry happen. But in those instances where you do have a fighting chance, you want to make sure of three key factors:

LISTEN

ENGAGE

REACT

If you remember to do those three things, you will be surprised at how ahead of the competition you will already be. Don't think about yourself. Don't think about your makeup or your outfit or where you have to be later in the day. Don't think about who is watching your audition or is it going on tape or will you get a second chance to read through or did they make changes to the copy. Just simply think about listening to the person standing next to you, reacting to what they're saying, and engaging with them, and the audience at home.

If you get stuck with a bad co-host, don't fret! It's not always such a bad thing. Sure, it's hard to connect and engage with someone who's just staring at the teleprompter like a zombie, or who doesn't react when you say something. But remember that in this instance, you have the chance to shine, to throw a life-preserver to your sinking co-host, and really show what an absolute professional you are. For example, if it's their turn to read and they don't, you can chime in with a line to help them back.

So let's take this copy below as an example. You are host 1.

(HOST 1)

HERE ON MAKEOVER IN A MINUTE, WE'RE GOING TO TEACH YOU SIMPLE TRICKS AND HINTS TO GET YOURSELF A FRESH NEW LOOK.

(HOST 2)

AND THIS ISN'T JUST FOR THE LADIES, YOU MEN OUT THERE COULD USE OUR ADVICE AS WELL. TRUST ME. SOME OF YOU COULD REALLY BENEFIT FROM LEARNING THE VALUE OF A PAIR OF TWEEZERS.

Now let's say that after reading your line, your co-host freezes. This is where you could throw the life-preserver, by jumping in there with "AND, JIM – WE'RE NOT ONLY TALKING ABOUT WOMEN RIGHT? WE'VE GOT SOMETHING FOR EVERYONE HERE?" And see if that helps "Jim" find his way out of his head and back to the copy. If it does – you are a hero. If it doesn't –

you could just continue, reading his line and waiting for him to return from outer space.

What this says to the casting director is this: YOU ARE A PRO. You know how to save your partner, and this person isn't even your partner! They're just someone auditioning with you! I cannot express how much of a positive light this shines on you. And so you see, you can still nail an audition even if your co-host doesn't.

CHAPTER SIX:

NAIL YOUR AUDITION

So now you've got your brand, you've made your reel, you're ready to rock and roll. You get a call for an audition – you can't believe it! Your day is here! You do the prep work, think about all the elements and how to balance those elements, you walk into the door of the audition and you see the camera, the casting director, the producer, and the lights. And you get dizzy. Your heart starts to race. You get up to do your read – and you bomb, big time. What just happened? YOU GOT STUCK IN YOUR HEAD. Repeat that after me. Because it happens all the time. It happens to nearly everyone. And you need to make sure it doesn't happen to you – again.

My first "trick" that I like to share with people is this: Do NOT drink coffee before an audition. I don't care if it's six o'clock in the morning and you feel totally dead and you're not going to survive without it. As soon as you walk into that room, your adrenaline is going to go through the roof. And there's nothing worse for an adrenaline rush than a caffeine rush. If you must, must, must have coffee first thing in the morning, make sure you're done with it at least 90 minutes before you audition. I promise you will thank me for this hint.

Now that you've shown up and your caffeine levels aren't through the roof and you've studied and prepared the copy and added your ISMs and your POV, now it's time to walk into the audition and kill it. Sometimes when you walk in, the producers and/or casting directors will ask you a series of questions about yourself. And these questions will range from, "Where are you from?" to "Where do you see yourself in 10 years?" So it's your job to have narrowed down exactly how to answer these questions quickly, concisely, with confidence and authority, and with your POV in it. What they don't want to hear is, "Um… well, let's see… where do I begin? I guess… I sort of grew up in the Midwest but we moved a lot… um…" They want to know you're smart, sharp and most importantly, that you know who you are. You're a pro. So an answer like "I grew up in the Midwest but we moved so often that it's hard to call one state home." See, you still got the same point across but without all the nervous ummms and ahhhhs. It's important for you to remember that your audition started the second you walked into the room. They are looking at everything about you, from the interview to the actual reading of the copy. So don't think you can dick around and stumble and stutter and that as long as your read is good you'll get the job, because you're wrong. You are SELLING yourself from the second you walk into the room until the second you leave.

Now that you've gotten all chatty, you should be a little more comfortable and ready to read. And now it's really time to shine. Take your deep breaths, remember to breathe, remember that punctuation in copy is not to be ignored (take your pauses where you see the commas), and most importantly: remember that YOU are the perfect person for this job, and that no one else can do better than you. Now... connect with your audience. Who are you talking to? Who is the demographic? Look into that camera and see the news junkie or the sports junkie or the music junkie or whoever that person is, and TALK TO THEM. Tell them the story. As you change from one topic to the next, use your transitions to transcend from one idea to the next. Smile. Breathe. And you will nail it.

This final part may seem completely ridiculous, but the only reason I give these specific tips is because they are things I've seen people do time and again when I've managed a casting or held an audition. You, like me, might think it's obvious that you shouldn't bring your dog to an audition. That you should wear makeup and brush your hair. That you shouldn't hike up your very low top while you're in the middle of a read, or that you shouldn't wear 6 dozen metal bangle bracelets that make your voice indecipherable over their jingling and jangling. But I see it all the time. ALL the time. Please, I implore you, don't be one these people. And if you're not, you're literally already halfway there.

CHAPTER SEVEN:

APPLYING WHAT YOU JUST LEARNED

This is the kind of book you need to read more than once. There's a lot of information in these pages, and it takes time for so much information to sink in. So let's recap, and put into motion what you have just learned. If you filled out the workbook section of "How to Find Your Brand," then hopefully you are now more comfortable with the seed you're going to plant in the TV soil. What you put your focus on *will* expand, I promise. You will watch your seed/brand grow as you water it with all of this knowledge. Once you have your brand down and you begin to create the materials needed to support it, your career can really take off.

Hosting is the one arena where you can actually shoot your materials on your own – create your own reel – and submit yourself for work. It's not only 100% acceptable, but it's really expected of you. You have no excuse not to go out and create your materials. If you really want to work in the hosting world, this is what's required of you. It's work. And you should really consider yourself lucky, because there's no other arena where you can really put yourself out there and do the work on your own and gain experience on your own, making yourself relevant and getting yourself work. Take acting, for example. You cannot just "create" an acting reel. You need to have legitimately worked as an actor to put on your reel. So think about how lucky you are to be able to create this on your own. But you can't really do it (successfully) until you figure out who you are and what your brand is. Sure, you can create a "generic hosting reel" but that's exactly what buyers are going to think when they watch it. If you don't stand out – if you don't have a brand, a personality, an ISM, then you're going to get tossed in the pile of "generic hosts." You know there's something special about you, so it's your job to get people to see it!

Hopefully this book has helped you discover what makes you stand out and what sets you apart. Now remember, discovering your brand is only the first step. As you grow, your brand will grow.

For example, let's say your brand starts out as a "party planner" and you create a great reel showing you giving party planning tips and tricks, and then you get engaged and plan your wedding, so you add a "webisodes" or "VLOG" with tips on how that... and then you get pregnant and decide to eat organic and go green so you add that as well... once the baby comes you decide to create an organic, sustainable nursery. And now, guess what? Your brand has now transformed into a green expert party and wedding planner – and you have the reel to prove it!

So now you have your brand, you have your reel, you're tweeting once a day (at least!) giving relevant information relating to your brand, and a weekly blog. And if you're asking, "Why do I have to write a blog if I'm doing all this other stuff?" The reason is simple: It keeps you relevant. Buyers still want to see your inner Carrie Bradshaw. Now coupled with all of this, you're doing your monthly webisodes based on your brand, and always with your point of view. Remember: it's 50% brand, 50% your opinion (which equals your point of view). One of my favorite sayings is, "Opinions are like assholes, we all have them." And you can't host without one, because brands can be redundant but your POV is yours, and yours alone. It's what makes you unique and different and it's what keeps your reel from being a "generic hosting reel." So, if you build it, they will come knocking. And now when they do come, you will be ready to recognize the elements, balance the elements and shine, shine, shine!

What you have now that others don't is this handy book. So many other hosts, or "wannabe" hosts have part of what you have: they've figured out their brand, built their materials and started to get traction. They got meetings lined up with agents and managers, they started to book auditions. But then they didn't know what to do when they walked into the audition or meeting. Now that you've read this book from cover to cover, you now know who you are and what you're selling in yourself and connecting to your audience because they are more important than you and when you put them before you – that's when you become the star of your show. And of your career. This book is just the beginning of the basic information. More books, more information to come.

ABOUT THE AUTHOR

Marki Costello is the owner and founder of Creative Management Entertainment Group, a company that manages more than 30 successful television hosts and brands. She also created and runs Hollywood's Premiere Hosting Academy, "Become a Host" and BECOMEAHOST.COM. She resides in Los Angeles with her two sons, Lucas and Finn, and her long-term boyfriend Tommy.

Made in the USA
Lexington, KY
31 October 2013